OWLS

BIRDS OF PREY

BY NATHAN SOMMER

EPIC

BELLWETHER MEDIA • MINNEAPOLIS, MN

EPIC BOOKS are no ordinary books. They burst with intense action, high-speed heroics, and shadows of the unknown. Are you ready for an Epic adventure?

This edition first published in 2019 by Bellwether Media, Inc.

No part of this publication may be reproduced in whole or in part without written permission of the publisher. For information regarding permission, write to Bellwether Media, Inc., Attention: Permissions Department, 6012 Blue Circle Dr. Minnetonka, MN 55343.

Library of Congress Cataloging-in-Publication Data

Names: Sommer, Nathan, author.
Title: Owls / by Nathan Sommer.
Description: Minneapolis, MN : Bellwether Media, Inc., 2019. | Series: Epic.
    Birds of Prey | Audience: Age 7-12. | Audience: Grade 2 to 7. | Includes
    bibliographical references and index.
Identifiers: LCCN 2018003578 (print) | LCCN 2018006818 (ebook) | ISBN
    9781626178816 (hardcover : alk. paper) | ISBN 9781681036281 (ebook)
Subjects: LCSH: Owls–Juvenile literature. | Birds of prey–Juvenile
    literature.
Classification: LCC QL696.S8 (ebook) | LCC QL696.S8 S66 2019 (print) | DDC
    598.9/7–dc23
LC record available at https://lccn.loc.gov/2018003578

Editor: Kate Moening   Designer: Josh Brink

Printed in the United States of America, North Mankato, MN.

TABLE OF CONTENTS

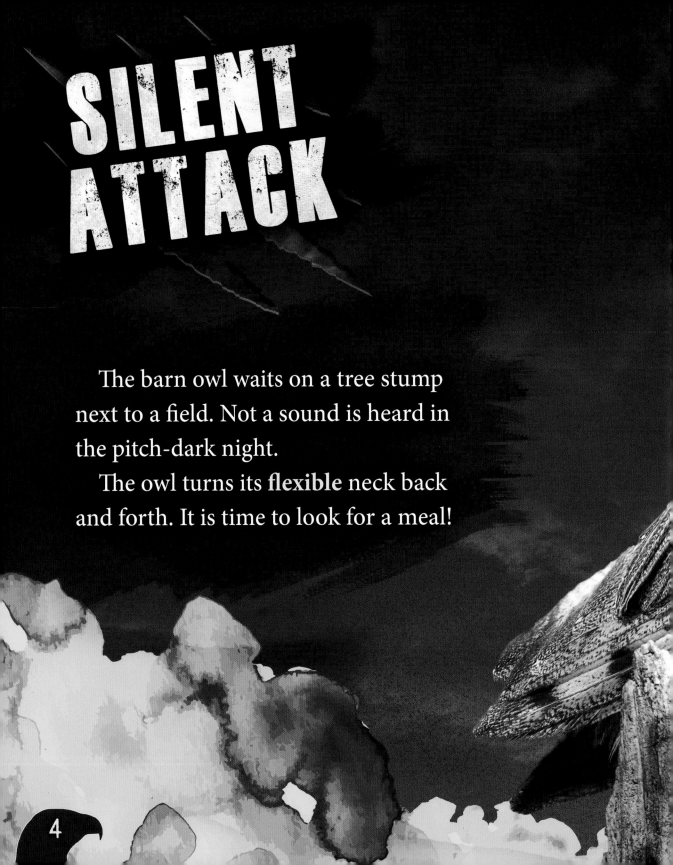

SILENT ATTACK

The barn owl waits on a tree stump next to a field. Not a sound is heard in the pitch-dark night.

The owl turns its **flexible** neck back and forth. It is time to look for a meal!

4

5

The owl hears a mouse scurrying across the field. The hungry **predator** quietly drops from its **perch**.

The owl's wings make no sound in the air.
Its silent flight takes its **prey** by surprise!

WHAT ARE OWLS?

EURASIAN EAGLE-OWL

Owls are birds of prey found around the world. They have short tails and rounded wings.

GREAT GRAY OWL

These predators have flat faces and large, rounded eyes. The biggest owls stand up to 2.5 feet (0.8 meters) tall.

Owls live in many **habitats**. They do not build nests. Instead, they steal holes and nests made by other animals!

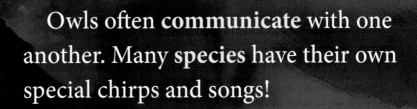

Owls often **communicate** with one another. Many **species** have their own special chirps and songs!

TYPES OF OWLS

BARN OWL

SNOWY OWL

GREAT GRAY OWL

BARRED OWL

HUNTING IN THE DARK

BLAKISTON'S FISH OWL

These **carnivores** are mostly **nocturnal**. They hunt at night. Some owls are more active at dawn and dusk.

Smaller species, like elf owls, munch on bugs. Larger species eat **rodents**. Eagle owls can take down foxes!

Owl vs. Owl

Larger owls often hunt smaller owls. Great horned owls are the barred owl's most common predator. Barred owls, in turn, eat smaller screech owls!

LITTLE OWL

Most owls hunt from branches, stumps, or rooftops. Others fly silently over fields to surprise prey below.

The birds swoop down quickly with open wings. They attack prey with their outstretched pointed **talons**.

TALONS

Many **adaptations** help owls hunt in darkness. Flat faces funnel sound to their ears. This helps them track down noises.

LONG-EARED OWL

Hearing It All

Nothing gets past owls. Some can hear a mouse stepping on a twig 75 feet (23 meters) away!

The birds' eyes are shaped like tubes instead of **spheres**. Their eyes remain stuck in one place. Their flexible necks help them look around!

BARRED OWL

Owls also have special feathers on their wings. These make the birds silent in flight.

Talons spread out as owls make a catch.
Prey rarely escapes these silent predators!

SNOWY OWL

19

GREAT HORNED OWL PROFILE

RED LIST STATUS: LEAST CONCERN

LEAST CONCERN	NEAR THREATENED	VULNERABLE	ENDANGERED	CRITICALLY ENDANGERED	EXTINCT IN THE WILD	EXTINCT

AVERAGE LIFE SPAN: ABOUT 13 YEARS

GREATEST HUNTING TOOLS: SILENT FLIGHT AND EXCELLENT HEARING

WINGSPAN: UP TO 4.8 FEET (1.5 METERS)

TOP SPEED: 40 MILES (64 KILOMETERS) PER HOUR

GREAT HORNED OWL RANGE MAP

GREAT HORNED OWL
RANGE =

PREY

SKUNKS	RABBITS	CHIPMUNKS	BATS

GLOSSARY

adaptations—changes in animals over time that make them better able to hunt and survive

carnivores—animals that only eat meat

communicate—to talk or share information

flexible—able to easily bend or twist in many directions

habitats—the homes or areas where animals prefer to live

nocturnal—active at night

perch—a high place where birds watch for prey, such as a branch or rooftop

predator—an animal that hunts other animals for food

prey—an animal that is hunted by another animal for food

rodents—small mammals that gnaw on their food; mice, squirrels, and beavers are all rodents.

species—different types of an animal based on size, color, and location; great horned owls are a species of owl.

spheres—ball-shaped objects

talons—the strong, sharp claws of owls and other birds of prey

TO LEARN MORE

At the Library

Hamilton, S.L. *Owls*. Minneapolis, Minn.: Abdo Pub., 2018.

Lawrence, Riley. *Snowy Owls of the Tundra*. New York, N.Y.: KidHaven Publishing, 2018.

O'Shaughnessy, Ruth. *Owls After Dark*. New York, N.Y.: Enslow Publishing, 2016.

On the Web

Learning more about owls is as easy as 1, 2, 3.

1. Go to www.factsurfer.com.

2. Enter "owls" into the search box.

3. Click the "Surf" button and you will see a list of related web sites.

With factsurfer.com, finding more information is just a click away.

INDEX

The images in this book are reproduced through the courtesy of: Fall-line Photography, cover; Ian Duffield, p. 2; Michael Shake, pp. 4-5; David Dirga, p. 6; Danita Delmont, p. 7; Hana Duncova, p. 8; Ondrej Prosicky, pp. 9, 21 (left middle); Nuwat Phansuwan, p. 10; MZPHOTO.CZ, p. 11 (top left); Collins93, p. 11 (top right); Glass and Nature, p. 11 (bottom left); Rob Stokes, p. 11 (bottom right); feathercollector, p. 12; Exactostock-1598, p. 13; Stanislav Duben, p. 14; HelloRF Zcool, p. 15; Mriya Wildlife, p. 16; effective stock photos, p. 17; critterbiz, p. 18; Daniel Dunca, p. 19; Imran Ashraf, p. 20; Heiko Kiera, p. 21 (left); RT Images, p. 21 (right middle); Jay Ondreicka, p. 21 (right).